JOURNEY

For all of you who have had to take "the journey." May you stay strong and true.

JOURNEY

designs by
Jane Richmond &
Shannon Cook

photography by
Nicholas Kupiak

MARIAN RAE PUBLICATIONS

Published in 2013 by MARIAN RAE PUBLICATIONS

ISBN 978-0-9917289-1-6

MARIAN RAE PUBLICATIONS

www.marianraepublications.com

CONTENTS

JANE

ISLAND took Shannon and I on an incredible journey. Being my first book there were so many firsts. Publishing a book is like planning a wedding: it takes over your life for the better part of a year, the stress can be insurmountable, deadlines are rock solid and deal breaking, and by the end you've spent so much time so close to the project it can be hard to see it with fresh eyes. But when the whirlwind is over and you can finally breathe again, the end result is so rewarding and tangible you almost forget how much work it was...

...that is, until you do it again! With JOURNEY, Shannon and I have combined our design efforts to bring you a book that represents both of our aesthetics rolled into one. If you know us (personally or online) or follow our work, you'll know that Shannon and I have very different personalities. I'm the minimalist: My style is classic, I love white on white (on white!), I think simple is better, and my designs often reflect this. On the other hand, Shannon has so much flare, she loves bright colors and fun patterns, she loves to layer prints, and she is constantly pushing the envelope with her modern, fashion-forward pieces. And together, like yin and yang, we work incredibly well together. Somehow our differences play off of each other in a way that perpetuates great productivity, efficiency, and creativity.

The theme of this collaboration was born from a road trip storyboard that was the brainchild of our talented photographer, Nicholas Kupiak. I think it took on a deeper meaning for both Shannon and I as we started to ponder the kinds of journeys that people embark on. There is a journey that only you can take, the kind that leads you back to yourself. The journey can be in search of balance, change, adventure, peace, love, or acceptance. It's the path that takes you back when you've been led astray. The road is often winding with ups and downs, bumps and even backtracking. All of these things are what make us who we are and in the end we need to embrace it all as part of the journey.

The inspiration for my three pieces – Climb, hiking socks; Spate, the fingerless mittens; and Inland, the tunic-length cardigan; was the need to be comfy and cozy. I wanted to design pieces that felt like comfort food on a damp and dreary day; pieces to live in. The kind of knitwear you would pack for that journey; pieces that would comfort you and prepare you for anything.

I really hope you enjoy this book and that it leaves you feeling confident about the JOURNEY you're on, the one you are ready to embark on, or the journey you took long ago that led you to where you are today.

jour.ney (jur-nee) : passage or progress from one stage to another

We all have a journey to make. One of self discovery, finding ourselves and the ability to fully embrace who we are. One of discovering inner strength, learning to love who we are, just as we are – faults and all. One of learning to trust our instincts, inner voice, and true self. That journey is never ending. We are always changing, growing and experiencing new paths.

This book has been quite the journey for me. I've stretched myself to learn new things, to think in new ways, and to trust my gut. I've realized it's okay to think differently and to see things in a unique way. I would never have been able to do that without Jane. She's been my partner-in-crime in what has been for me a creative and personal journey of my own self-discovery. Jane's been there with me every step of the way and I couldn't ask for a better friend in life. I wouldn't stay up so late at night for just anyone. We've worked hard, all the while laughing, crying, finding balance in our health (we both have weird, strict diets and newfound addictions to health food and green smoothies), supporting each other and just plain going through life's journey together this past year.

After Jane and I released ISLAND last fall, we knew we had to do another book. That journey was special and so is this one–just in a different way. This time we decided to produce a joint collection of patterns. Merging our design aesthetics has been so much fun. It's brought together what we feel is a special book.

We all are on a journey. Where our paths go may be different, but the thing that holds us all together is that we all take one path or another. The moral of the story is that we all need to believe in and love who we are–both in life and in our creative passions.

So indulge…grab some of that special yarn you've been holding onto, curl up with JOURNEY and reflect. Take some time to lose yourself in the images, the designs, the paths…and knit. Let go of the daily stresses and all the baggage we carry everyday. Just be you. Feel the yarn between your fingers, the calming movement of your needles clicking away, and just let go…let us take you…on a JOURNEY.

Happy knitting from my home to yours.

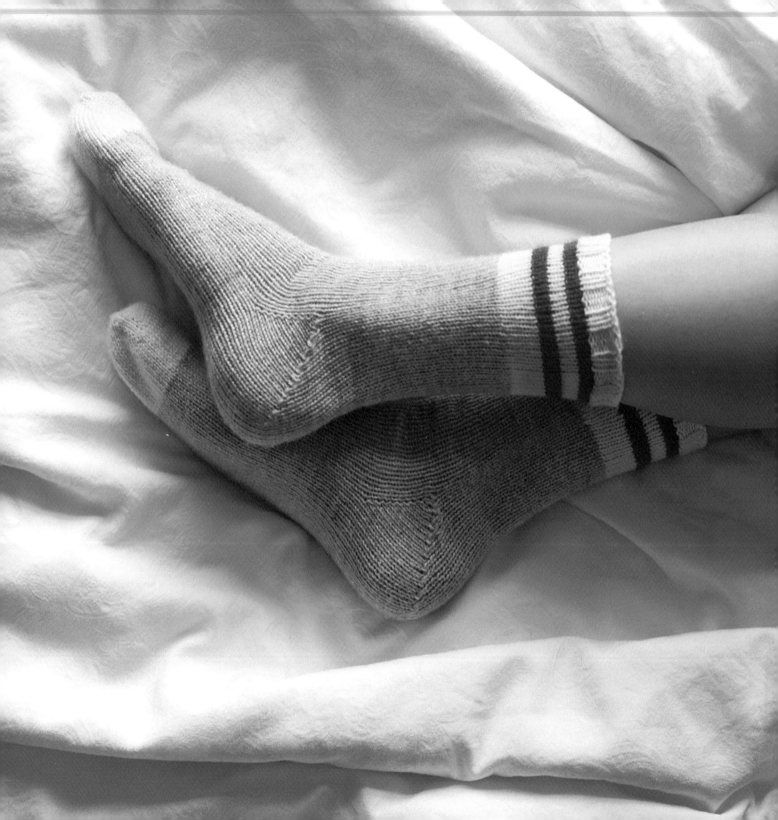

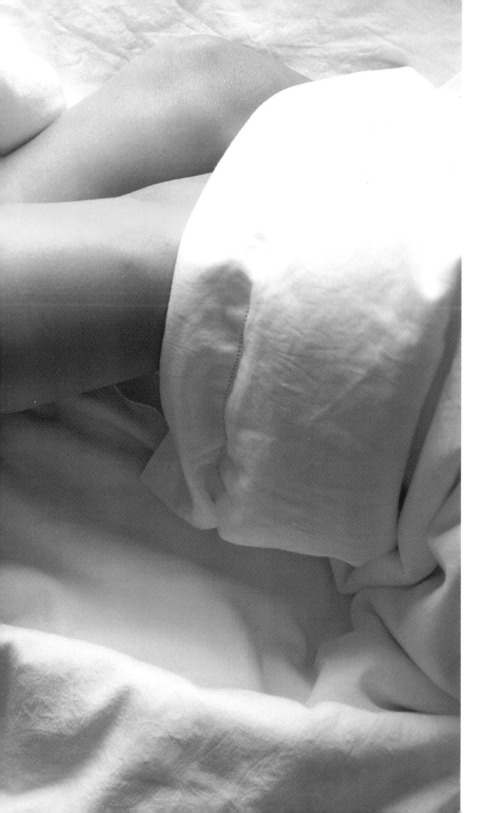

CLIMB
page 80

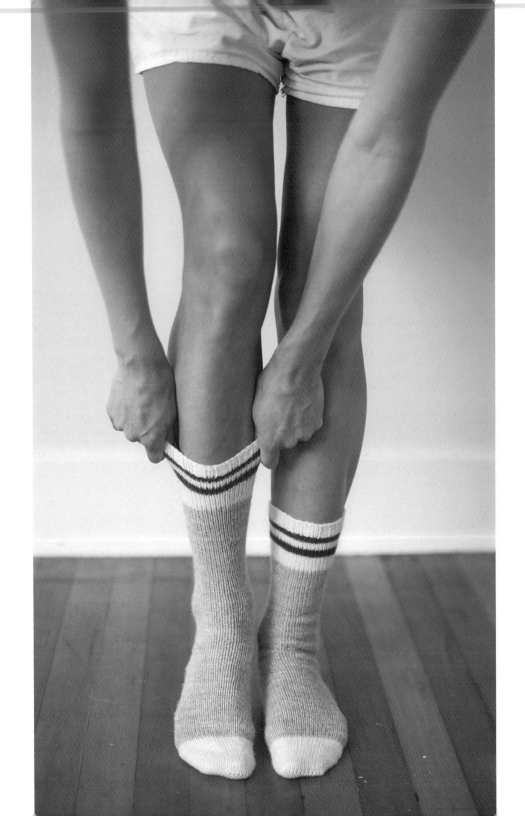

ONWARD

page 82

SPATE

page 86

SWIFT
page 88

ANTRORSE

page 90

INLAND

page 100

THE PATTERNS

CLIMB
by Jane Richmond

Simple socks knit from the toe up and inspired by classic work socks.

Gauge

30 sts and 44 rows = 4in/10cm in St st in the rnd

Finished Measurements

5.75 (6.5, 7.25)in/14.5 (16.5, 18.5) cm foot circumference (unstretched)

Sizes

To fit 8 (9, 9.75)in/20.5 (23, 25.5) cm foot circumference (at instep), sample is 9in/23cm

Yarn

Main Colour
2 balls of Knit Picks Stroll Fingering (75% Superwash Merino, 25% Nylon, 211m/231yds per 50g/1.76oz ball), shown in Dove Heather [fingering]

Toe Colour
40g of Knit Picks Bare (75% Superwash Merino, 25% Nylon, 422m/462yds per 100g/3.53oz skein) [fingering]

Stripe Colour
15g of Knit Picks Stroll Fingering (75% Superwash Merino, 25% Nylon, 211m/231yds per 50g/1.76oz ball), shown in Firecracker Heather [fingering]

Needles

2.75mm/US2 dpns or long circular needle if using magic loop

Adjust needle size if necessary to obtain the proper gauge.

Notions

Yarn needle
Removable marker

PATTERN NOTES

Measure your instep and choose your size based on the foot circumferences listed above. A handy chart referencing standard **Foot Measurements** is listed on the following page if you are knitting for someone other than yourself and need guidance when selecting a size.

Please note that negative ease is built into the pattern and does not need to be subtracted from the size you select.

My favorite socks to knit and wear have a slightly looser fabric than traditional hand knit socks. This produces a nice stretchy fabric that I find really comfortable to wear as well as fun and fast to knit, it should be noted that socks knit at a looser gauge are not as hard wearing as socks knit at a tighter gauge. Because these socks are meant to stretch around the foot they will look long and narrow while you are knitting them.

STITCH GUIDE

M1R: Insert LH needle from back to front under the horizontal bar between the two needles, knit through the front of the lifted stitch.

M1L: Insert LH needle from front to back under the horizontal bar between the two needles, knit through the back of the lifted stitch.

DIRECTIONS

TOE

Using **Turkish Cast-On** method and **Toe Colour**, CO 10 (12, 12) sts each needle for a total of 20 (24, 24) sts.

If working on dpns, put 10 (12, 12) sts on first needle for sole of foot, and divide rem 10 (12, 12) across 2 needles for instep. If using a long circular, keep 10 (12, 12) on each needle.

You may wish to place a removable marker in fabric to mark beginning of rnd as the tail ends up on the opposite end of the rnd after working the **Turkish Cast-On**.

Rnd 1 (Inc Rnd): [K1, M1R, knit to last sole/instep st, M1L, k1] twice. 4 sts increased.

Rnd 2: Knit.

Repeat **Rnds 1 & 2** until there are 44 (48, 52) sts total.

Knit 10 rnds more in *Toe Colour*. Change to *Main Colour* and knit until foot measures 1.5(1.75, 1.75)in /4 (4.5, 4.5)cm less than the desired length of foot from tip of toe to back of heel. See **Standard Foot Measurements** chart.

HEEL

Shape Gusset

Rnd 1: K1, M1R, knit to last sole st, M1L, k1, knit to end of rnd.

Rnd 2: Knit.

Repeat **Rnds 1 & 2** until there are 38 (42, 46) sole sts.

Turn Heel

The second half of the heel is worked flat across the sole sts only.
Row 1 (RS): Knit to the last 2 sole sts, turn.

Row 2 (WS): Sl1, p18 (20, 22), p2tog, p1, turn.

Row 3: Sl1, k5, ssk, k1, turn.

Row 4: Sl1, p6, p2tog, p1, turn.

Row 5: Sl1, k7, ssk, k1, turn.

Row 6: Sl1, p8, p2tog, p1, turn.

Row 7: Sl1, k9, ssk, k1, turn.

Row 8: Sl1, p10, p2tog, p1, turn.

Row 9: Sl1, k11, ssk, k1, turn.

Continue as established until all sts are worked and there are 22 (24, 26) sole sts left, ending with a **RS** row. Knit across the remainder of rnd (across instep sts).

44(48, 52) total sts.

LEG

Knit until leg measures 2.5in/6.5cm short of desired length.

Knit 10 rnds using *Toe Colour*.
Knit 5 rnds using *Stripe Colour*.
Knit 5 rnds using *Toe Colour*.
Knit 5 rnds using *Stripe Colour*.
Knit 1 rnd using *Toe Colour*.

Work in **2 x 2 Ribbing** for 9 rnds.

Bind off loosely using the **Sewn Bind-Off** method (see page 116).

STANDARD FOOT MEASUREMENTS	Ladies			Men		
	S	M	L	M	L	XL
Inches						
Foot Circumference	8	8	9	8	9	9.75
Sock Height	7	7.25	7.5	7.5	8	8.5
Total Foot Length	9	10	11	10.5	11	11.5
Centimeters						
Foot Circumference	20.5	20.5	23	20.5	23	25.5
Sock Height	17.5	18.5	19	19	20.5	21.5
Total Foot Length	23	25.5	28	26.5	28	29

ONWARD
by Shannon Cook

This modern shawl showcases a lovely, textured, reversible pattern that is sure to catch your eye. It's knit in worsted-weight yarn that's perfect to cozy up in when the weather is cool. You'll find this pattern (and the easy-to-memorize format) a fun knit!

Gauge

17 sts and 27 rows = 4in/10cm in St st (blocked)

Yarn

6 skeins Quince and Co. Lark (100% American wool, 134yds/123m per 50g skein), shown in Glacier [worsted]

Needles

4.5mm/US7 needle–long circular recommended

Notions

1 removable marker
4 stitch markers
Yarn needle
Waste yarn

Finished Measurements

Approx wingspan 66in/167.75cm and 32.5in/82.75cm deep after blocking.

STITCH GUIDE

Lace Bind-Off: To work the bind off knit the first 2 stitches together through the back loops. Next slip the stitch on your right-hand needle back to your left-hand needle purlwise. Repeat the above steps until you have 1 stitch left. Cut your yarn and pull through your last stitch.

PATTERN GUIDE

#1 - 1ST ARROW DIRECTION

Row 1 (WS): K1, [k6, p6] to 1 st before m, k1, sm, k1, sm, k1, [p6, k6] to last st, k1.

Row 2 (RS): K1, sm, yo, p5, [k6, p6] to 2 sts before m, p2, yo, sm, k1, sm, yo, p2, [k6, p6] to 5 sts before m, p5, yo, sm, k1. (4 sts increased)

Row 3: [K6, p6] to 4 sts before m, k4, sm, k1, sm, k4, [p6, k6] to end.

Row 4: K1, sm, yo, p4, [k6, p6] to 5 sts before m, p5, yo, sm, k1, sm, yo, p5, [k6, p6] to 4 sts before m, p4, yo, sm, k1. (4 sts increased)

Row 5: K5, [p6, k6] to 1 st before m, p1, sm, k1, sm, p1, [k6, p6] to last 5 sts, k5.

Row 6: K1, sm, yo, p3, [k6, p6] to 2 sts before m, k2, yo, sm, k1, sm, yo, k2, [p6, k6] to 3 sts before m, p3, yo, sm, k1. (4 sts increased)

Total of 12 sts increased for this section.

PATTERN NOTES

This pattern has a "moving repeat" throughout. Please keep this in mind while you are reading the instructions. Onward is written with an easy-to-follow format that doesn't require chart knitting. Once you start knitting, you will find the pattern quick to memorize and simple to read your work. Comprised of knit and purl stitches, Onward is designed to be a relaxing knit.

#2 - ARROW BOXES

Row 1 (WS): K5, [p6, k6] to 3 sts before m, p3, sm, k1, sm, p3, [k6, p6] to last 5 sts, k5.

Row 2 (RS): K1, sm, yo, k4, [p6, k6] to 3 sts before m, p3, yo, sm, k1, sm, yo, p3, [k6, p6] to 4 sts before m, k4, yo, sm, k1. (4 sts increased)

Row 3: K1, p5, [k6, p6] to 4 sts before m, k4, sm, k1, sm, k4, [p6, k6], to last 6 sts, p5, k1.

Row 4: K1, sm, yo, k5, [p6, k6] to 4 sts before m, p4, yo, sm, k1, sm, yo, p4, [k6, p6] to 5 sts before m, k5, yo, sm, k1. (4 sts increased)

Row 5: K1, [p6, k6] to 5 sts before m, k5, sm, k1, sm, k5, [p6, k6] to last st, k1.

Row 6: K1, sm, yo, [k6, p6] to 5 sts before m, p5, yo, sm, k1, sm, yo, p5, [k6, p6] to m, yo, sm, k1. (4 sts increased)

Total of 12 sts increased for this section.

#3 - 2ND ARROW DIRECTION

Row 1 (WS): K1, p1, [k6, p6] to m, sm, k1, sm, [p6, k6] to last 2 sts, p1, k1.

Row 2 (RS): K1, sm, yo, k2, [p6, k6] to 5 sts before m, k5, yo, sm, k1, sm, yo, k5, [p6, k6] to 2 sts before m, k2, yo, sm, k1. (4 sts increased)

Row 3: K1, p4, [k6, p6] to 5 sts before m, p5, sm, k1, sm, p5, [k6, p6] to last 5 sts, p4, k1.

Row 4: K1, sm, yo, k5, [p6, k6] to 4 sts before m, k4, yo, sm, k1, sm, yo, k4, [p6, k6] to 5 sts before m, k5, yo, sm, k1. (4 sts increased)

Row 5: K2, [p6, k6] to 4 sts before m, p4, sm, k1, sm, p4, [k6, p6] to last 2 sts, k2.

Row 6: K1, sm, yo, p2, [k6, p6] to 3 sts before m, k3, yo, sm, k1, sm, yo, k3, [p6, k6] to 2 sts before m, p2, yo, sm, k1. (4 sts increased)

Total of 12 sts increased for this section.

#4 - GARTER

Row 1 (WS): Knit.

Row 2 (RS): K1, sm, yo, knit to m, yo, sm, k1, sm, yo, knit to m, yo, sm, k1. (4 sts increased)

Rows 3-6: Repeat **Row 1 & 2** twice.

Total of 12 sts increased for this section.

DIRECTIONS

Slip all markers as you come to them throughout the pattern.

Using the **Long-Tail Method** CO 3 sts.

Rows 1 (RS): K1, yo, k1, yo, k1. Place removable marker on this side to denote RS. (5 sts)

Row 2 (WS): Knit.

Rows 3: [K1, yo] twice, pm, k1, pm, yo, k1, yo, k1. (9 sts)

Row 4: Knit.

Row 5: K1, pm, yo, k to m, yo, sm, k1, sm, yo, k to last st, yo, pm, k1. (13 sts)

Row 6: K across.

Row 7: K1, sm, yo, k to m, yo, sm, k1, sm, yo, k to m, yo, sm, k1. (17 sts)

Row 8: K across.

Repeat **Rows 7 & 8** eight times more ending on **Row 8**. (49 sts)

Row 25: Repeat **Row 7**. (53 sts)

Follow the **Pattern Guide** for the rest of the pattern starting with **#1 - 1st Arrow Direction** and work your way through all of the sections to the end of **#4 - Garter**.

Repeat the **4 sections** in the **Pattern Guide** 5 times more or until 64.5in/164cm wingspan and 30.5in/77.5cm depth or desired size.

Repeat the first 4 rows of section **#4 - Garter.** (Shawl shown has 6 repeats of the Pattern Guide, 349 sts after final 4 rows of garter.)

BO using **Lace Bind-Off**. Wet block to measurements.

SHAWL MAP - RIGHT WING SPAN SHOWN

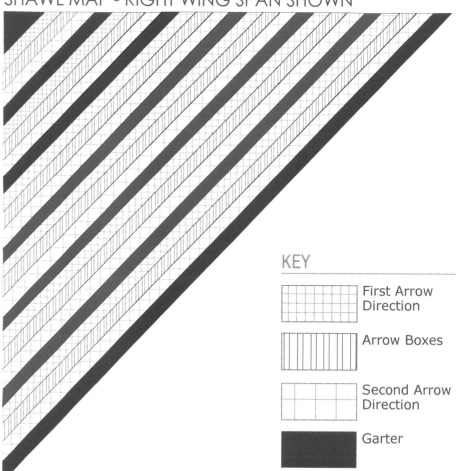

KEY

First Arrow Direction
Arrow Boxes
Second Arrow Direction
Garter

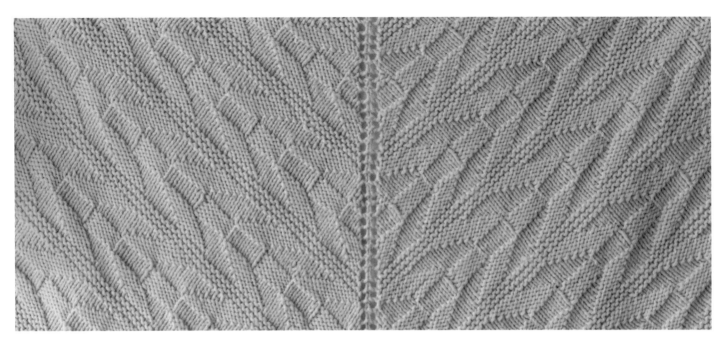

Use the following stitch counts as a guide along the way.

PATTERN GUIDE STITCH COUNTS

1ST PATTERN REPEAT STITCH COUNT

End of **1st Arrow Direction**   65 sts

End of **Arrow Boxes**   77 sts

End of **2nd Arrow Direction**   89 sts

End of **Garter**   101 sts

2ND PATTERN REPEAT STITCH COUNT

End of **1st Arrow Direction**   113 sts

End of **Arrow Boxes**   125 sts

End of **2nd Arrow Direction**   137 sts

End of **Garter**   149 sts

3RD PATTERN REPEAT STITCH COUNT

End of **1st Arrow Direction**   161 sts

End of **Arrow Boxes**   173 sts

End of **2nd Arrow Direction**   185 sts

End of **Garter**   197 sts

4TH PATTERN REPEAT STITCH COUNT

End of **1st Arrow Direction**   209 sts

End of **Arrow Boxes**   221 sts

End of **2nd Arrow Direction**   233 sts

End of **Garter**   245 sts

5TH PATTERN REPEAT STITCH COUNT

End of **1st Arrow Direction**   257 sts

End of **Arrow Boxes**   269 sts

End of **2nd Arrow Direction**   281 sts

End of **Garter**   293 sts

6TH PATTERN REPEAT STITCH COUNT

End of **1st Arrow Direction**   305 sts

End of **Arrow Boxes**   317 sts

End of **2nd Arrow Direction**   329 sts

End of **Garter**   341 sts

SPATE

by Jane Richmond

The texture on these mitts creates an intriguing all-over raindrop pattern that is deceivingly simple to knit and requires no cable needle. Spate features a fold-able cuff that can be worn flipped over your fingers to keep them warm on those blustery days. These are sure to become your staple mitts.

Gauge

18 sts and 26 rows = 4in/10cm in St st on smaller needles

21 sts and 28 rnds = 4in/10cm in pattern stitch on smaller needles (in the rnd and blocked)

Yarn

1 skein Sincere Sheep Bannock (100% Targhee wool, 256m/280yds per 113g/4oz skein), shown in Cumulus [worsted]

Sample used 147m/161yds

Needles

4.5mm/US7 dpns or long circular needle
5mm/US8 dpns or long circular needle

Adjust needle size if necessary to obtain the proper gauge.

Notions

Removable marker
Yarn needle

Sizes

XS–S (M–L)

Finished Measurements

Approx 11.75in/30cm long and 6.75 (7.5)in/15 (16.5)cm hand circumference (unstretched).

STITCH GUIDE

LT : Insert RH needle into back of second st on LH needle and knit st through back loop, leave st on needle, k2tog tbl, slip both sts off of needle.

RT : K2tog leaving sts on needle, knit first st, slip both sts off of needle.

DIRECTIONS

FOREARM

2 x 2 Ribbing

Using **Long-Tail Method** and larger needles, CO 36 (40) sts. Join, being careful not to twist. You may wish to place a removable marker in fabric to mark beginning of rnd.

Rnd 1: [P1, k2, p1] to end of rnd.

Repeat **Rnd 1** until ribbing measures 2in/5cm.

Pattern Stitch

Rnd 1: [RT, LT] to end of rnd.

Rnds 2-4: [K1, p2, k1] to end of rnd.

Rnd 5: [LT, RT] to end of rnd.

Rnds 6-8: [P1, k2, p1] to end of rnd.

Repeat **Rnds 1-8.** When mitten measures 4.5in/11.5cm, change to smaller needles and continue in pattern until mitten measures 7.75in/19.5cm from CO edge, ending with **Rnd 1**.

THUMB OPENING

The thumb opening is made by working flat rather than in the round. Make thumb opening as follows:

Turn, so that **WS** is facing.

Row 1 (WS): [P1, k2, p1] to end of rnd, turn.

Row 2 (RS): [K1, p2, k1] to end of rnd, turn.

Row 3: Repeat **Row 1**.

Row 4: [LT, RT] to end of rnd, turn.

Row 5: [K1, p2, k1] to end of rnd, turn.

Row 6: [P1, k2, p1] to end of rnd, turn.

Row 7: Repeat **Row 5**.

Row 8: [RT, LT] to end of rnd, rejoin for working in the rnd.

HAND

Rnds 1-3: [K1, p2, k1] to end of rnd.

Rnd 4: [LT, RT] to end of rnd.

Rnds 5-7: [P1, k2, p1] to end of rnd.

Rnd 8: [RT, LT] to end of rnd.

2 x 2 Ribbing

Rnd 1: [K1, p2, k1] to end of rnd.

Repeat **Rnd 1** until ribbing measures 1.5in/4cm.

BO loosely in rib.

Weave in ends. Wet block and lay flat to dry to open up the stitch pattern.

SWIFT

by Shannon Cook

Featuring a geometric lace pattern with textural details and fun angular lines, the Swift hat is as enjoyable to knit as it is to wear.

Gauge

24 sts and 34 rnds = 4in/10cm in St st on larger needles, in the rnd

29 sts and 36 rnds = 4in/10cm in pattern on larger needles, in the rnd

Yarn

2 skeins Quince and Co. Chickadee (100% American wool, 181yds/166m per 50g skein), shown in Clay [sport]

Needles

3mm/US2.5 circular needle, 16 in (for ribbing)

3.5mm/US4 circular needle, 16in, (for working body of hat)

3.5mm/US4 dpns, long circular or 2 short circulars (for working crown decrease)

Adjust needle size if necessary to obtain correct gauge.

Notions

1 stitch marker
Yarn needle

Finished Measurements

Approx 18in/45cm circumference (unstretched) and 9.75in/24.5cm long, blocked.

DIRECTIONS

RIBBING

Using **Long-Tail Method** and smaller needles, CO 124 sts. Place marker and join, being careful not to twist.

Rnd 1: [K2, p2] to end of rnd.

Repeat **Rnd 1** until ribbing measures approx 1.5in/3.5cm.

BODY

Change to larger circular (16in) needles.

Set Up Rnd: [K62, m1] twice. (126 sts)

Work **Lace Pattern** repeat (from **Chart** or written instructions below) two times, ending with **Rnd 32**. Hat should measure approx 9in/22cm from CO edge.

LACE PATTERN

Rnd 1 and all odd rnds: [Yo, k5, sl 1, k2tog, psso, k5, yo, k1] to end of rnd.

Rnds 2, 4, 6, 8, & 10: Knit.

Rnds 12 & 14: Purl.

Rnds 16, 18, 20, 22, 24, 26, & 28: Knit.

Rnds 30 & 32: Purl.

SHAPE CROWN

When circumference gets too small to work comfortably on 16in needle, switch to dpns/long circular/2 short circulars, as you prefer.

Rnd 1: [K1, k2tog] to end of rnd. (84 sts)

Rnds 2, 4 & 6: Knit.

Rnd 3: [K2tog] to end of rnd. (42sts)

Rnd 5: [K2tog] to end of rnd. (21sts)

Cut yarn, leaving a 6-inch tail. Use yarn needle to thread end through remaining sts. Pull tight and tie off.

Weave in ends and wet block your hat.

LACE PATTERN CHART

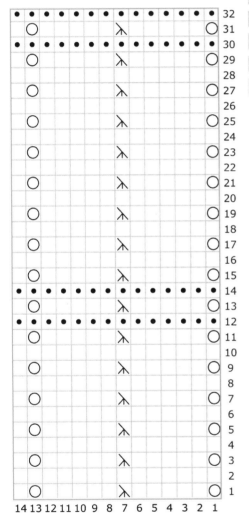

KEY

☐ knit

○ yo

⅄ sl1, k2tog, psso

• purl

☐ repeat around

ANTRORSE

by Shannon Cook

Antrorse is your new favorite pullover. Featuring a cozy reversible funnel neck that can be worn open or buttoned, this pullover delivers comfort with a modern edge. The center panel adds a fun detail that draws the eye upward - it's slimming and fun to knit!

Gauge

15.5 sts and 22 rows = 4in/10cm in St st

14 sts and 32 rows = 4in/10cm in garter stitch

Yarn

Quince & Co. Osprey (100% wool, 155m/170yds to 100g/3.5oz skein), shown in Birds Egg
[aran]

See page 98 to determine the number of skeins required

Needles

6mm/US10 circular needle, 32in
6mm/US10 dpns or long circular needle

Notions

1 removable marker
6 stitch markers
Cable needle
Yarn needle
Waste yarn
Large buttons
(approx 1⅛in/3cm)

PATTERN NOTES

This pullover is intended to be worn with 2in/5cm of positive ease, please choose your size accordingly. The pullover is knit top down, worked flat & then joined in the round once the funnel neck portion is completed.

HOW TO USE THIS PATTERN

This pullover is knit from the top down. To offer a wide range of sizes and maintain readability, this pattern is written with blank spaces so that you may input only the information pertaining to your size.

Here is how to use this pattern:

1. Choose Your Size

Refer to the **Finished Measurements & Yarn Requirements** chart on page 98. Select your size based on the **Bust Size** measurements found at the top of the chart. If you prefer a looser or tighter fit choose a different size, using the **Finished Measurements** listed to guide you (sample is shown in size 32).

2. Find Your Size

Refer to the **Pattern Chart** on page 96. Mark or highlight the column that contains the instructions for the size you have chosen.

3. Fill In The Blanks

Pencil in the numbers given in the **Pattern Chart** with the corresponding letters in the written pattern.

NOTE: Measurements are listed in inches and centimeters and larger spaces are provided so that you may include the unit of measurement within the space.

4. Pattern Guide

Use the **Pattern Guide** on pages 94 & 95 for your **Center Panel Pattern**, certain **Increase Rounds**, and **Sleeve Separation Round**.

STITCH GUIDE

M1 (EZ's Backwards Loop Version): Simply make a loop using the **Backwards Loop Cast-On Method** (see page 111) onto your right needle and on the next row treat the loop as a separate stitch. Take care to pull the stitch nice and tight so it blends in.

M1L (make one left): With left needle tip, lift strand between needles from front to back. Knit lifted loop through the back. This will make a left-slanting increase.

M1R (make one right): With left needle tip, lift strand between needles from back to front. Knit lifted loop through the front. This will make a right-slanting increase.

SSK (slip, slip, knit): Slip the next 2 sts, individually, as if to knit, onto the right needle. Insert left needle into the front loops of the slipped stitches and knit them together (through the back loops). This makes a left-slanting decrease.

1RBH (One-Row Buttonhole):

1. Work to buttonhole, wyif sl 1st purl wise. Wyib, *slip next st from left needle. Pass the first slipped st over it; rep from * three times more (not moving yarn). Slip the last bound-off stitch to left needle and turn your work.

2. Using the **Cable Cast-On Method** (see page 111), wyib, CO 5 sts as follows: *Insert the right needle between the first and second stitches on the left needle, draw up a loop, place the loop on the left needle; repeat from the * four times more, turn your work.

3. Wyib, sl the first stitch from the left needle and pass the extra cast-on st over it to close the buttonhole. Work to the end of the row as per pattern.

DIRECTIONS

FUNNEL NECK

Using **Long-Tail Method** and circular needle CO 97 sts.

Rows 1-7: Knit.

Row 8 (WS): K16, M1L, pm, k1, pm, M1R, k44, M1L, pm, k1, pm, M1R, k35 to end of row. (101 sts)

Rows 9 & 10: Knit.

Row 11 (RS): Knit to last 7 sts, work **1RBH**, k2.

Row 12: K2, ktbl 5 times, knit.

Row 13: Knit to last 7 sts, ktbl 5 times, k2.

Rows 14 & 15: Knit.

Row 16 (Inc Row): Knit to m, M1L, sm, k1, sm, M1R, knit to next m, M1L, sm, k1, sm, M1R, knit to end. (105 sts)

Rows 17-20: Knit.

Row 21: Knit to last 7 sts, work **1RBH**, k2.

Rows 22 & 23: Repeat **Rows 12 & 13.**

Row 24 (Inc Row): Knit to m, M1L, sm, k1, sm, M1R, knit to next m, M1L, sm, k1, sm, M1R, knit to end. (109 sts)

Rows 25-30: Knit.

Row 31: Knit to last 7 sts, work **1RBH**, k2.

Row 32 (Inc Row): K2, ktbl for 5sts, knit to m, M1L, sm, k1, sm, M1R, knit to next m, M1L, sm, k1, sm, M1R, knit to end. (113 sts)

Row 33: Rep **Row 13**.

Row 34-39: Knit.

Row 40 (Inc Row): Knit to m, M1L, sm, k1, sm, M1R, knit to next m, M1L, sm, k1, sm, M1R, knit to end. (117 sts)

Row 41: For **Sizes 30-42** knit. **Sizes 44-50** knit to last 7sts, work **1RBH**, k2.

Sizes 30-42 continue to **Yoke - Set Up Rnd 1**.

Sizes 44-50 continue on to **Row 42**.

Rows 42 & 43: Repeat **Rows 12 & 13**.

Rows 44-47: Knit.

Row 48: Knit to m, M1L, sm, k1, sm, M1R, knit to next m, M1L, sm, k1, sm, M1R, knit to end. (121 sts)

Row 49: Knit.

YOKE

Rnd 1 (Set Up Rnd): Slip 7 sts onto stitch holder from the end of the row **without live yarn**. Pm and join in round (this will be the 8th stitch in) making sure that your **RS is facing you**, being careful not to twist work. Purl across to last 7 sts. Place the 7 sts that are on your stitch holder onto a cable needle and hold to back of work. *Wyif sl next st on left needle purlwise to right-hand needle, sl next st from cable needle purlwise to right-hand needle. Slip 2 sts from right-hand needle to left. P2tog. Repeat from * 6 more times. 110 (110, 110, 110, 110, 110, 110, 114, 114, 114, 114) sts.

Rnd 2: Knit (A) _____ sts, *k2, m1; rep from * until end of rnd removing markers as you go. (B) _____ sts.

Rnd 3: Knit (C) _____ sts, work **Rnd 1** of CPP, pm, knit to end of rnd.

Rnd 4: Knit (C) _____ sts, work **Rnd 2** of CPP, knit to end of rnd.

Rnd 5: For **Sizes 30 & 32** work in pattern as set to marker (**Rnd 3** of CPP), then work **Inc Rnd 1**. (D) _____ sts. **All other sizes** work in pattern as set to marker (**Rnd 3** of CPP), knit to end of rnd.

Rnd 6: For **Sizes 34, 36, 38, 40, 42, 44, 46, 48, 50**, work in pattern as set to marker (**Rnd 4** of CPP), then work **Inc Rnd 1**. (D) _____ sts. **All other sizes** knit to end of rnd.

Rnd 7: Work in pattern as set to marker (**Rnd 5** of CPP), knit to end of rnd.

Rnd 8: Work in pattern as set to marker (**Rnd 6** of CPP), knit to end of rnd.

Rnd 9: Work in pattern as set to marker (**Rnd 7** of **CPP**), knit to end of rnd.

Rnd 10: For **Sizes 30 & 32** work to marker in pattern as set, work **Rnd 8** of **CPP** then work **Inc Rnd 2**. (E) _____ sts. **All other sizes** work in pattern as set to marker (**Rnd 8 of CPP**), knit to end of rnd.

Rnd 11: Work in pattern as set to marker (**Rnd 9** of **CPP**), knit to end of rnd.

Rnd 12: For **Sizes 34, 36, 38, 40, 42, 44, 46, 48, 50**, work in pattern as set to marker (**Rnd 10** of **CPP),** then work **Inc Rnd 2**. (E) _____ sts. **All other sizes** work in pattern as set to marker (**Rnd 10** of **CPP**), knit to end of rnd.

Rnd 13: Work in pattern as set to marker (**Rnd 11** of **CPP**), knit to end of rnd.

Rnd 14: Work in pattern as set to marker (**Rnd 12** of **CPP**), knit to end of rnd.

Rnd 15: For **Sizes 30 & 32** work in pattern as set to marker (**Rnd 13** of **CPP**), then work **Inc Rnd 3**. (F) ____ sts. **All other sizes** work in pattern as set to marker (**Rnd 13** of **CPP**), knit to end of rnd.

For **Size 30** work **Sleeve Separation Round** then continue knitting starting at **Rnd 17**. (L) _____ total body sts.

Rnd 16: Work in pattern as set to marker (**Rnd 14** of **CPP**), knit to end of rnd.

Rnd 17: Work in pattern as set (**Rnd 15** of **CPP**), knit to end of rnd.

For **Size 32** work **Sleeve Separation Round** then continue knitting starting at **Rnd 19**. (L) _____ total body sts.

Rnd 18: For **Sizes 34, 36, 38, 40, 42, 44, 46, 48, 50**, work in pattern as set to marker (**Rnd 16** of **CPP**), then work **Inc Rnd 3**. (F) _____ sts. **All other sizes** knit to end of rnd.

For **Size 34** work **Sleeve Separation Round** then continue knitting starting at **Rnd 20**. (L) _____ total body sts.

Rnd 19: Work in pattern as set to marker (**Rnd 17** of **CPP**), knit to end of rnd.

For **Sizes 36, 38, 40, 42, 44, 46, 48, 50**, work **Sleeve Separation Round** then cont knitting starting at **Rnd 21**. (L) _____ total body sts.

Rnd 20: Work in pattern as set to marker (**Rnd 18** of **CPP**), knit to end of rnd.

BODY

Rnd 21: Work in pattern as set to marker (**Rnd 19** of **CPP**), knit to end of rnd.

Continue as established repeating **Rnds 2-19** of **CPP** until pullover measures approx (M) _____ from top of funnel.

HEM

Remove marker denoting start of rnd, continue as established (also removing your CPP marker) and work around until the approx side of sweater is reached, place marker (denoting new start of rnd), purl to end of rnd.

Continue working in **garter stitch** in the rnd approx 3in/7cm or desired length. BO.

SLEEVES

Place (N) _____ sts onto long circular or dpns. Rejoin yarn, pick up and knit (O) _____ sts along CO edge of underarm, placing a marker at center of cast on stitches to denote beginning of rnd. Join. (P) _____ total sleeve sts.

Work **St st** for 2in/5cm.

Next Rnd (Dec Rnd): K1, k2tog, knit to last 3 sts of rnd, ssk, k1.

Work **Dec Rnd** every (Q) _____ until (R) _____ sleeve sts remain.

Work even until sleeve measures (S) _____ from underarm or desired length.

Work in **garter stitch** in the rnd for 2in/5cm. BO.

Weave in ends and close holes at underarms if necessary. Block garment according to schematic on page 99. Once dry sew on your buttons.

PATTERN GUIDE

Use the following sections as directed in the pattern directions on pages 92 and 93.

CPP (CENTER PANEL PATTERN)

Rnd 1: P9, k1, p9.

Rnd 2 & all even rnds: Knit.

Rnd 3: P8, k3, p8.

Rnd 5: P7, k5, p7.

Rnd 7: P6, k7, p6.

Rnd 9: P5, k4, p1, k4, p5.

Rnd 11: P4, k4, p3, k4, p4.

Rnd 13: P3, k4, p5, k4, p3.

Rnd 15: P2, k4, p7, k4, p2.

Rnd 17: P1, k4, p9, k4, p1.

Rnd 19: K4, p5, k1, p5, k4.

Rep **Rnds 2-19** for **Center Panel Pattern**.

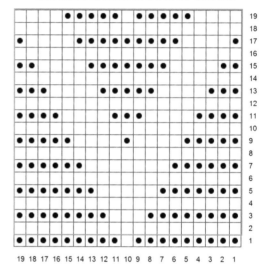

CENTER PANEL PATTERN CHART

KEY

● Purl

☐ Knit

*Please note the following rounds DO NOT include the stitches worked for the Center Panel Pattern.

INCREASE ROUND 1

Sizes 30, 32 & 40: *K29 (16, 7), m1; rep from * 3 (7, 19) more times, k to end of round. You will now have (D) _____ sts.

Size 34: K17, *m1, k10; rep from * 11 times more, k to end of rnd. You will now have (D) _____ sts.

Size 36: *K8, m1; rep from * 15 times more, k to end of rnd. You will now have (D) _____ sts.

Size 38: *K8, m1; rep from * 16 times more, k to end of rnd. You will now have (D) _____ sts.

Size 42: K12, m1, *k5, m1; rep from * 24 times more, k to end of rnd. You will now have (D) _____ sts.

Size 44: *K5, m1; rep from * 27 times more, k to end of rnd. You will now have (D) _____ sts.

Size 46: K16, *m1, k4; rep from * 29 times more, k to end of rnd. You will now have (D) _____ sts.

Size 48: *K4, m1; rep from * 34 times more, k to end of rnd. You will now have (D) _____ sts.

Size 50: K17, *m1, k3; rep from * 38 times more, k to end of rnd. You will now have (D) _____ sts.

INCREASE ROUND 2

Sizes 30 & 32: K39 (22), m1, *k35 (18), m1; rep from * 2 (6) more times, knit to end of rnd. You will now have (E) _____ sts.

Size 34: *K12, m1; rep from * 11 times more, knit to end of rnd. You will now have (E) _____ sts.

Size 36: K17, m1, *k9, m1; rep from * 14 times more, knit to end of rnd. You will now have (E) _____ sts.

Size 38: *K9, m1; rep from * 16 times more, knit to end of rnd. You will now have (E) _____ sts.

Size 40: K16, m1, *k7, m1; rep from * 19 times more, knit to end of rnd. You will now have (E) _____ sts.

Size 42: K13, m1, *k6, m1; rep from * 24 times more, knit to end of rnd. You will now have (E) _____ sts.

Size 44: K19, m1, *k5, m1; rep from * 27 times more, knit to end of rnd. You will now have (E) _____ sts.

Size 46: K19, *m1, k5; rep from * 29 times more, knit to end of rnd. You will now have (E) _____ sts.

Size 48: *K5, m1; rep from * 34 times more, knit to end of rnd. You will now have (E) _____ sts,

Size 50: K18, m1, *k4, m1; rep from * 37 times more, knit to end of rnd. You will now have (E) _____ sts.

INCREASE ROUND 3

Sizes 32, 36 & 44: K21 (18, 8), m1, *k17 (10, 7), m1; rep from * 6 (14, 27) more times, knit to end of rnd. You will now have (F) _____ sts.

Size 30: K39, m1, *k37, m1; rep from * 2 times more, knit to end of rnd. You will now have (F) _____ sts.

Size 34: *K13, m1; rep from * 11 times more, knit to end of rnd. You will now have (F) _____ sts.

Size 38:*K9, m1; rep from * 17 times more, knit to end of rnd. You will now have (F) _____ sts.

Size 40: K17, m1, *k8, m1; rep from * 19 times more, knit to end of rnd. You will now have (F) _____ sts.

Size 42: K14, m1, *k7, m1; rep from * 24 times more, knit to end of rnd. You will now have (F) _____ sts.

Size 44: K20, m1, *k6, m1; rep from * 27 times more, knit to end of rnd. You will now have (F) _____ sts.

Size 46: K18, m1, *k6, m1; rep from * 28 times more, knit to end of rnd. You will now have (F) _____ sts.

Size 48: K22, m1, *k5, m1; rep from * 34 times more, knit to end of rnd. You will now have (F) _____ sts.

Size 50: K16, m1, *k5, m1; rep from * 38 times more, knit to end of rnd. You will now have (F) _____ sts.

SLEEVE SEPARATION ROUND

Knit (C) _____ sts, work next rnd of **CPP**, knit (G) _____ sts, place (H) ___ sts on waste yarn, CO (I) ___ sts using **Backwards Loop Cast-On**, knit (J) ___ sts, place (H) ___ sts on waste yarn, CO (I) ___ sts using **Backwards Loop Cast-On**, knit (K) ___ sts.

PATTERN CHART

To Fit Bust	in	30	32	34	36	38	40	42	44	46	48	50
	cm	76	81.5	86.5	91.5	96.5	102	107	112	117	122	127
Pullover Increases												
A	Stitches at Start of Set Up Round	2	2	2	2	2	2	2	6	6	6	6
B	Stitches after Set Up Round	164	164	164	164	164	164	164	168	168	168	168
C	Stitches before Center Panel	0	0	0	0	0	0	0	4	4	4	4
D	Total Stitches after 1st Increase Round	168	172	176	180	181	184	190	196	198	203	207
E	Total Stitches after 2nd Increase Round	172	180	188	196	198	205	216	225	228	238	246
F	Total Stitches after 3rd Increase Round	176	188	200	212	216	226	242	254	258	274	286
Separate Sleeves from Body												
G	Stitches after CPP and before 1st Sleeve Separation	18	19	21	23	24	26	28	30	31	33	35
H	Sleeve Stitches Separated	33	37	39	41	41	42	46	48	48	52	54
I	Underarm Stitches	7	8	8	9	9	10	10	11	11	12	12
J	Stitches between Sleeves	55	57	61	65	67	71	75	79	81	85	89
K	Stitches after 2nd Sleeve Separation to End of Round	18	19	21	23	24	26	28	30	31	33	35
Body												
L	Total Body Stitches	124	130	138	148	152	162	170	184	188	198	206
M	Body Length from Top of Funnel to Start of Hem	in	21.25	21.5	21.75	22	22.25	22.25	22.5	22.5	22.75	23	23
		cm	54	55	55.5	56	56.5	56.5	57	57	58	58.5	58.5
Sleeves												
N	Sleeve Stitches to Pick Up	33	37	39	41	41	42	46	48	48	52	54
O	Stitches to Pick Up for Underarm	7	8	8	9	9	10	10	11	11	12	12
P	Total Sleeve Stitches	40	45	47	50	50	52	56	59	59	64	66
Q	Decrease Round Interval	in	1.75	1.5	1.5	1.25	1.25	1.25	1	1	1	1	0.75
		cm	4.5	4	4	3	3	3	2.5	2.5	2.5	2.5	2
R	Total Sleeve Stitches after Decreases	26	29	29	30	30	32	32	35	35	36	36
S	Sleeve Length from Underarm before Cuff	in	15.5	15.5	16	16	16	16	16.5	16.5	16.5	16.5	16.5
		cm	39.5	39.5	41	41	41	41	42	42	42	42	42

FINISHED MEASUREMENTS &
YARN REQUIREMENTS

Bust Size	in	30	32	34	36	38	40	42	44	46	48	50
	cm	76	81.5	86.5	91.5	96.5	102	106.5	112	117	122	127
Yarn Requirements												
Number of 100g skeins (155m/170yds)		5	6	6	7	7	7	8	8	8	9	9
Meters Required		756	823	883	940	973	1026	1094	1153	1196	1261	1309
Yards Required		827	901	966	1029	1065	1123	1197	1262	1308	1380	1432
Number of Buttons		3	3	3	3	3	3	3	4	4	4	4
Finished Measurements (in)												
A	Bust/Hip Circumference	32	33.75	35.75	38.25	39.25	42	44	47.5	48.75	51.25	53.25
B	Total Body Length	24.25	24.5	24.75	25	25.25	25.25	25.5	25.5	25.75	26	26
C	Body Length (from underarm)	13.75	13.75	14	14	14.25	14.25	14.5	14.5	14.75	15	15
D	Arm Circumference	10.25	11.5	12	13	13	13.5	14.5	15.25	15.25	16.5	17
E	Sleeve Length (from underarm)	17.5	17.5	18	18	18	18	18.5	18.5	18.5	18.5	18.5
Finished Measurements (cm)												
A	Bust/Hip Circumference	81.5	86	91	97.5	100	107	112	121	124	130.5	135.5
B	Total Body Length	62	62.5	63	63.5	64	64	65	65	65.5	66.5	66.5
C	Body Length (from underarm)	35	35.5	35.5	35.5	36	36	37	37	37.5	38	38
D	Arm Circumference	27	29	30.5	33.5	33.5	34.5	37	38.5	38.5	42	43.5
E	Sleeve Length (from underarm)	44.5	44.5	46	46	46	46	47	47	47	47	47

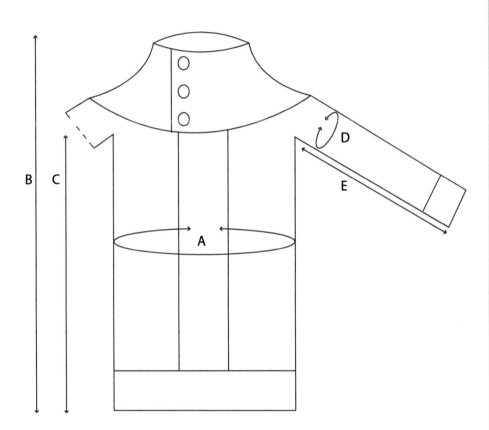

Finished measurements listed on page 98.

INLAND

by Jane Richmond

A reverse stockinette stitch body is divided by figure-slimming ribbing along the sides and front bands. The tunic length and afterthought pockets up the comfy factor on this roomy top-down cardigan. This simple knit works up quickly in chunky yarn. The single ply of Quince and Co's Puffin lends a lightness to the fabric, for an outer layer that isn't too heavy.

Gauge

12 sts and 17 rows = 4in/10cm in St st on smaller needle

Yarn

Quince & Co Puffin (100% American Wool, 112yds/102m per 100g skein), shown in Frost
[bulky]

See page 106 to determine the number of skeins required

Needles

6.5mm/US10.5 circular needle, 32in
6.5mm/US10.5 dpns or long circular needle
8mm/US11 circular needle, 24in

Notions

4 stitch markers
1 removable marker
Waste yarn
Yarn needle
Large buttons (approx 1⅛in/3cm)

HOW TO USE THIS PATTERN

This cardigan is knit from the top down. To offer a wide range of sizes and maintain readability, this pattern is written with blank spaces so that you may input only the information pertaining to your size. Here is how to use this pattern:

1. Choose Your Size

Refer to the **Finished Measurements & Yarn Requirements** chart on page 106 to select your size (sample shown in size 32 with 1in/2.5cm of positive ease).

2. Find Your Size

Refer to the **Pattern Chart** on page 105. Mark or highlight the column that contains the instructions for the size you have chosen.

3. Fill In The Blanks

Pencil in the numbers given in the **Pattern Chart** with the corresponding letters in the written pattern.

NOTE: Measurements are listed in inches and centimeters and larger spaces are provided so that you may include the unit of measurement (in/cm) within the space.

DIRECTIONS

COLLAR

Using **Long-Tail Method** and larger circular needle CO (A)_____ sts, casting on loosely to allow the collar to lay flat.

Row 1 (WS): Sl 1 purlwise, [p1, k1] to last 2 sts, p2.

Row 2 (RS): Sl 1 knitwise, [k1, p1] to last 2 sts, k2.

Repeat **Rows 1 & 2** until ribbing measures 6.25in/16cm, ending with a **WS** row.

YOKE

Change to smaller circular needle.

Row 1 (Set Up Row) (RS): Sl 1 knitwise, [k1, p1] twice, k1, purl (B)_____, pm, k1, kfb, k2, kfb, k2, pm, purl (C)_____, pm, k1, kfb, k2, kfb, k2, pm, purl (B)_____, k1, [p1, k1] twice, k1. 4 sts increased.

Row 2 (WS): Sl 1 purlwise, p1, [k1, p1] twice, *knit to last st before marker, kfb, sm, purl to marker, sm, kfb, repeat from * once more, knit to last 6 sts of row, [p1, k1] twice, p2. 4 sts increased.

Row 3: Sl 1 knitwise, [k1, p1] twice, k1, *purl to next marker, sm, k1, kfb, knit to 3 sts before marker, kfb, k2, sm, repeat from * once more, purl to last 6 sts of row, [k1, p1] twice, k2. 4 sts increased.

Row 4 (BO for Buttonhole): Sl 1 purlwise, p1, BO 2, p1, *knit to last st before marker, kfb, sm, purl to marker, sm, kfb, repeat from * once more, knit to last 6 sts of row, [p1, k1] twice, p2. 4 raglan sts increased; 2 buttonhole sts bound off.

Row 5 (CO for Buttonhole): Sl 1 knitwise, [k1, p1] twice, k1, *purl to marker, sm, k1, kfb, knit to 3 sts before marker, kfb, k2, sm, repeat from * once more, purl to last 4 sts of row, k1, p1, CO 2 using backwards loop method, k2. 4 raglan sts increased; 2 buttonhole sts cast on.

Continue to make **Two-Row Buttonholes** beginning on **WS** rows, the entire length of the body, spaced 3.5in/9cm apart or every _____ rows (based on your swatch). Omit raglan

increases (kfb) once yoke has been completed.

*Mark buttonhole on **RS** of work with a removable marker. This will serve as a reminder. Move your marker as you make each additional buttonhole.*

Row 6 (WS): Sl 1 purlwise, p1, [k1, p1] twice, *knit to last st before marker, kfb, sm, purl to marker, sm, kfb, repeat from * once more, knit to last 6 sts of row, [p1, k1] twice, p2. 4 sts increased.

Row 7 (RS): Sl 1 knitwise, [k1, p1] twice, k1, *purl to marker, sm, k1, kfb, knit to 3 sts before marker, kfb, k2, sm, repeat from * once more, purl to last 6 sts of row, [k1, p1] twice, k2. 4 sts increased.

Repeat **Rows 6 & 7** until there are:

(D)_____ front sts, (E)_____ sts each sleeve, (F)_____ back sts. (G)_____ total yoke sts.

Work even until cardigan measures (H)_____ from back neck at base of collar, ending with a **WS** row.

For Sizes 28.25, 31, 32.25, 35, and 36.25 Only:

Next Row (Separate sleeves from body) (RS): Sl 1 knitwise, [k1, p1] twice, k1, *purl to marker, sm, using backwards loop method, CO (I)_____ sts, place (E)_____ sleeve sts onto waste yarn, sm, repeat from * once more, purl to last 6 sts of row, [k1, p1] twice, k2.

For Sizes 39, 41, 43.75, 45, 47, and 48.25 Only:

Next Row (Separate sleeves from body) (RS): Sl 1 knitwise, [k1, p1] twice, k1, *purl to marker, remove marker, place (E)_____ sleeve sts onto waste yarn, using backwards loop method, CO (I)_____ sts, placing markers after first 2 CO sts and before last 2 CO sts (leaving 5 sts between your markers), repeat from * once more, purl to last 6 sts of row, [k1, p1] twice, k2.

For All Sizes:

(J)_____ total body sts.

BODY

Next Row (WS): Sl 1 purlwise, p1, [k1, p1] twice, *knit to marker, sm, p1, [k1, p1] twice, sm, repeat from * once more, knit to last 6 sts of row, [p1, k1] twice, p2.

Next Row (RS): Sl 1 knitwise, [k1, p1] twice, k1, *purl to marker, sm, k1, [k1, p1] twice, sm, repeat from * once more, purl to last 6 sts of row, [k1, p1] twice, k2.

Work even in **reverse St st**, maintaining ribbing as established by last 2 rows, until garment measures 4in/10cm from CO sts at underarm, ending with a **RS** row.

Waist Shaping

Next Row (Dec Row) (WS): Sl 1 purlwise, p1, [k1, p1] twice, *knit to 2 sts before marker, ssk, sm, work ribbing as established, sm, k2tog, repeat from * once more, knit to last 6 sts of row, [p1, k1] twice, p2. 4 sts decreased.

Work even for 3in/7.5cm, repeat **Dec Row** once more.

(K)_____ total body sts.

Work even until cardigan measures (L)_____ from CO sts at underarm, ending with a **RS** row.

Hip Shaping

Next Row (Inc Row) (WS): Sl 1 purlwise, p1, [k1, p1] twice, *knit to last st before marker, kfb, sm, p1, [k1, p1] twice, sm, kfb, repeat from * once more, knit to last 6 sts of row, [p1, k1] twice, p2. 4 sts increased.

Work even, repeating **Inc Row** every 2in/5cm three times more.

(M)_____ total body sts.

Work even until there are (N)_____ buttonholes, ending on a **CO for Buttonhole (RS)** row. Cardigan should measure approx (O)_____ from CO sts at underarm.

Ribbing

For Sizes 28.25, 31, 36.25, 39, 41, 43.75, 47 Only:

Next Row (Inc Row)(WS): Sl 1 purlwise, p1, [k1, p1] to marker, m1, sm, p1, [k1, p1] twice, sm, k1, [p1, k1] to marker, sm, p1, [k1, p1]

twice, sm, m1, [p1, k1] to last st of row, p1. 2 sts increased.

Next Row (RS): Sl 1 knitwise, k1, [p1, k1] to last st of row, k1.

For All Sizes:

Next Row (WS): Sl 1 purlwise, p1, [k1, p1] to last st of row, p1.

Next Row (RS): Sl 1 knitwise, k1, [p1, k1] to last st of row, k1.

Continue in **1 x 1 Ribbing** until one more buttonhole has been made, work even for 1in/2.5cm.

BO very loosely in rib.

Sleeves

Place (E)_____ sleeve sts onto dpns or long circular. Rejoin yarn, pick up and knit (P)_____ sts along CO edge of underarm, placing a marker at center of cast on stitches to denote beg of rnd. Join.

(Q)_____ total sleeve sts.

Knit for 3in/7.5cm from underarm.

Next Rnd (Dec Rnd): K1, k2tog, knit to last 3 sts of rnd, ssk, k1. 2 sts decreased.

Work **Dec Rnd** every (R)_____ until (S)_____ sleeve sts remain.

Work even until sleeve measures (T)_____ from underarm.

Next Rnd: K2tog, knit to end of rnd. 1 st decreased.

Work in **1 x 1 Ribbing** for 3in/7.5cm.

BO loosely in rib.

POCKETS

Right Pocket

With **RS** facing, using smaller circular needle and beginning at ribbing of right buttonhole band and ending at ribbing along right side of body, pick up and knit (U)_____ sts in the purl bumps of the row above ribbing at hem.

Next Row (WS): Purl.

Next Row (RS): Knit.

Continue in Stockinette stitch for 2.25in/5.5cm, ending with a **RS** row.

Next Row (Dec Row)(WS): Purl to last 3 sts of row, p2tog, p1. 1 st decreased.

Repeat **Dec Row** every 2.25in/5.5cm, twice more.

AT THE SAME TIME

Continue in Stockinette stitch until pocket measures approx 4.5in/11.5cm, ending with a **RS** row.

Next Row (WS): BO (V)_____ sts, purl to end of row.

Next Row (RS): Knit.

Next Row: Slipping first st, BO 2 sts, purl to end of row. 2 sts decreased.

Next Row: Knit.

Repeat last two rows until all sts have been bound off.

Left Pocket

With **RS** facing, using smaller circular needle and beginning at ribbing along left side of body and ending at left button band, pick up and knit (U)_____ sts in the purl bumps in the row above the ribbing at hem.

Next Row (WS): Purl.

Next Row (RS): Knit.

Continue in Stockinette stitch for 2.25in/5.5cm, ending with a **RS** row.

Next Row (Dec Row)(WS): P1, p2tog, purl to end of row. 1 st decreased.

Repeat **Dec Row** every 2.25in/5.5cm, twice more.

AT THE SAME TIME

Continue in Stockinette stitch until pocket measures approx 4.5in/11.5cm, ending with a **WS** row.

Next Row (RS): BO (V)_____ sts, knit to end of row.

Next Row (WS): Purl.

Next Row: Slipping first st, BO 2 sts, knit to end of row. 2 sts decreased.

Next Row: Purl.

Repeat last two rows until all sts have been bound off.

FINISHING

Attach sides of pockets by seaming along ribbing at sides of body and front bands. Weave in ends and close holes at underarms if necessary. Sew buttons to left front button band corresponding with buttonholes.

Block garment according to schematic on page 107.

To Fit Bust		in	28	30	32	34	36	38	40	42	44	46	48
		cm	71	76	81.5	86.5	91.5	96.5	101.5	106.5	112	117	122
Yoke													
A	Cast On		59	59	59	59	59	59	65	65	65	67	67
B	Purl		7	7	7	7	7	7	9	9	9	9	9
C	Back Neck		19	19	19	19	19	19	21	21	21	23	23
D	Front Stitches (each side)		22	24	25	27	28	28	30	32	33	34	35
E	Sleeve Stitches (each sleeve)		25	29	31	35	37	37	37	41	43	45	47
F	Back Stitches		37	41	43	47	49	49	51	55	57	61	63
G	Total Yoke Stitches		131	147	155	171	179	179	185	201	209	219	227
H	Raglan Depth	in	6.25	6.5	6.75	7	7.25	7.5	7.75	8	8.5	9	9.5
		cm	16	16.5	17	18	18.5	19	19.5	20.5	21.5	23	24
I	Cast On at Underarm		5	5	5	5	5	9	9	9	9	9	9
Body													
J	Total Body Stitches		91	99	103	111	115	123	129	137	141	147	151
K	Total Body Stitches at Waist		83	91	95	103	107	115	121	129	133	139	143
L	Work Even	in	10	10	10	10	10	9.75	9.75	9.5	9.25	8.75	8.5
		cm	25.5	25.5	25.5	25.5	25.5	25	25	24	23.5	22	21.5
M	Total Body Stitches (at full hip)		99	107	111	119	123	131	137	145	149	155	159
N	Buttonholes		8	8	8	8	9	9	9	9	9	9	9
O	Work Even	in	19.25	19	18.75	18.5	21.75	21.5	21.25	21	20.5	20	19.5
		cm	49	48.5	47.5	47	55	54.5	54	53.5	52	51	49.5
Sleeves													
P	Cast On at Underarm		6	6	6	6	6	10	10	10	10	10	10
Q	Total Sleeve Stitches		31	35	37	41	43	47	47	51	53	55	57
R	Decrease Round Interval	in	13.5	4.5	3.5	2.25	2.25	1.75	2	1.5	1.5	1.5	1.25
		cm	34.5	11.5	9	5.5	5.5	4.5	5	4	4	4	3
S	Total Wrist Stitches		27	27	27	27	29	29	31	31	33	33	33
T	Sleeve Length (to underarm)	in	16.5	16.5	17	17	17	17	17.5	17.5	17.5	17.5	18
		cm	42	42	43	43	43	43	44.5	44.5	44.5	44.5	45.5
Pockets													
U	Pick Up and Knit		19	21	21	23	25	25	27	29	29	31	31
V	Bind Off		3	5	5	7	9	9	11	13	13	15	15

FINISHED MEASUREMENTS & YARN REQUIREMENTS

To Fit Bust		in	28	30	32	34	36	38	40	42	44	46	48
		cm	71	76	81.5	86.5	91.5	96.5	101.5	106.5	112	117	122
Yarn Requirements													
Number of 100g skeins (102m/112yds)			7	8	8	9	10	11	11	12	12	13	13
Meters Required			690	796	796	863	960	1031	1079	1152	1187	1237	1282
Yards Required			758	874	874	948	1055	1132	1185	1265	1304	1359	1408
Number of Buttons			9	9	9	9	10	10	10	10	10	10	10
Finished Measurements (in)													
A	Bust		28.25	31	32.25	35	36.25	39	41	43.75	45	47	48.25
B	Waist Circumference		25.5	28.25	29.5	32.25	33.5	36.25	38.25	41	42.25	44.25	45.5
C	Hip		31.5	34.25	34.75	37.5	39.5	42.25	44.25	47	47.5	50.25	50.75
D	Body Length		30	30	30	30	33.5	33.5	33.5	33.5	33.5	33.5	33.5
E	Raglan Depth		6.25	6.5	6.75	7	7.25	7.5	7.75	8	8.5	9	9.5
F	Hem to Armhole		23.75	23.5	23.25	23	26.25	26	25.75	25.5	25	24.5	24
G	Arm Circumference		10.25	11.75	12.25	13.75	14.25	15.75	15.75	17	17.75	18.25	19
H	Sleeve Length (from underarm)		19.5	19.5	20	20	20	20	20.5	20.5	20.5	20.5	21
I	Back Neck		6.25	6.25	6.25	6.25	6.25	6.25	7	7	7	7.75	7.75
J	Wrist		7.25	7.25	7.25	7.25	7.75	7.75	8.25	8.25	8.75	8.75	8.75
Finished Measurements (cm)													
A	Bust		72	78.5	82	89	92.5	99	104	111	114.5	119.5	123
B	Waist Circumference		65	71.5	75	82	85.5	92	97	104	107.5	112.5	116
C	Hip		80	87	88.5	95.5	100.5	107.5	112.5	119.5	120.5	127.5	129
D	Body Length		76	76	76	76	85	85	85	85	85	85	85
E	Raglan Depth		16	16.5	17	18	18.5	19	19.5	20.5	21.5	23	24
F	Hem to Armhole		60	59.5	59	58	66.5	66	65.5	64.5	63.5	62	61
G	Arm Circumference		26	29.5	31.5	34.5	36.5	40	40	43	45	46.5	48.5
H	Sleeve Length (from underarm)		42	42	43	43	43	43	44.5	44.5	44.5	44.5	45.5
I	Back Neck		16	16	16	16	16	16	18	18	18	19.5	19.5
J	Wrist		18.5	18.5	18.5	18.5	19.5	19.5	21	21	22.5	22.5	22.5

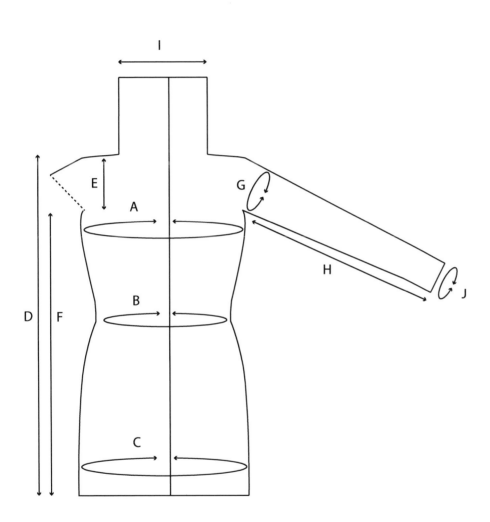

Finished measurements listed on page 106.

RESOURCES

Quince and Co.
www.quinceandco.com

Sincere Sheep
www.sinceresheep.com

Knit Picks
www.knitpicks.com

ABBREVIATIONS

approx	approximately		**pm**	place marker
beg	beginning		**psso**	pass slipped st over
BO	bind-off		**p2tog**	purl 2 sts together
CC	contrasting colour		**p3tog**	purl 3 sts together
cn	cable needle		**rem**	remaining
CO	cast-on		**RH**	right-hand
dec	decrease		**rnd(s)**	round(s)
dpns	double pointed needles		**RS**	right side
inc	increase		**RT**	right twist
k	knit		**skp**	slip 1, k1, psso
kfb	knit through front and back		**sk2p**	slip 1, k2tog, psso
k2tog	knit 2 sts together		**sl**	slip
k3tog	knit 3 sts together		**sm**	slip marker
LH	left-hand		**sp2p**	slip 1, p2tog, psso
LT	left twist		**ssk**	slip, slip, knit slipped sts together
m	marker		**st(s)**	stitch(es)
MC	main colour		**St st**	Stockinette stitch
M1	make one		**tbl**	through back loop
M1L	make one left		**WS**	wrong side
M1R	make one right		**wyib**	with yarn in back
p	purl		**wyif**	with yarn in front
patt	pattern		**yo**	yarn over
pfb	purl through front and back		**1RBH**	One-Row Buttonhole

BACKWARDS LOOP CAST-ON (during knitting): With stitches on your right needle, wrap working yarn around your left index finger from back to front. Insert tip of needle under front of loop on finger. Remove finger and pull yarn gently to snug loop around needle. Take care not to make your loops too tight but not too loose either.

CABLE CAST-ON: Turn your work so the wrong side (or inside) is facing you. Insert your right needle between the first and second stitch on your left needle and knit a stitch like normal, do not remove any stitches from the left needle. Without twisting it, slip the stitch from your right needle to the left needle. This is your first cast on stitch. Repeat these steps until you have cast-on the desired number of stitches.

GARTER STITCH: *Flat* - Knit every row. *In the Round* - Knit on the RS and purl on the WS.

LACE BIND-OFF: To work the bind off knit the first 2 stitches together through the back loops. Next slip the stitch on your right needle back to your left needle purlwise. Repeat the above steps until you have 1 stitch left. Cut your yarn and pull it through your last stitch.

LONG-TAIL CAST-ON: See page 114.

M1 (EZ's Backwards Loop Version) Simply make a loop using the **Backwards Loop Cast-On Method** onto your right needle and on the next row treat the loop as a separate stitch. Take care to pull the stitch nice and tight so it blends in. 1 st increased.

M1L (make one left): With left needle tip, lift strand between needles from front to back. Knit lifted loop through the back. 1 st increased. This will make a left-slanting increase.

M1R (make one right): With left needle tip, lift strand between needles from back to front. Knit lifted loop through the front. 1 st increased. This will make a right-slanting increase.

SEWN BIND-OFF: See page 116.

STOCKINETTE STITCH (St st): *Flat* - Knit on the RS and purl on the WS. *In the Round* - Knit every round.

SSK (slip, slip, knit): Slip the next 2 sts, individually, as if to knit, onto the right needle. Insert left needle into the front loops of the slipped stitches and knit them together (through the back loops). 1 st decreased. This makes a left-slanting decrease.

TURKISH CAST-ON: See page 112.

1RBH (One-Row Buttonhole):

1. Work to buttonhole, wyif sl 1st purl wise. Wyib, *slip next st from left needle. Pass the first slipped st over it; rep from * three times more (not moving yarn). Slip the last bound-off stitch to left needle and turn your work.

2. Using the **Cable Cast-On Method**, wyib, CO 5 sts as follows: *Insert the right needle between the first and second stitches on the left needle, draw up a loop, place the loop on the left needle; repeat from the * four times more, turn your work.

3. Wyib, sl the first stitch from the left needle and pass the extra cast-on st over it to close the buttonhole. Work to the end of the row as per pattern.

SPECIAL TECHNIQUES

TURKISH CAST-ON

For the Turkish Cast-On you will need one long circular needle.

1. Holding the needle tips parallel to each other with your right hand and with tips facing the same direction, place a slip knot on the top needle and begin wrapping the yarn around both needles.

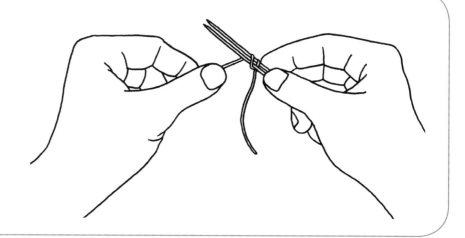

2. Without counting the slip knot, make half as many wraps as required cast on stitches. For example, if you require a total of 24 stitches you will need to wrap your yarn 12 times.

3. Turn the needles 180 degrees so that the top needle with the slip knot is now on the bottom, hold with your left hand and with your right pull the bottom needle so that the wraps are sitting on the cable.

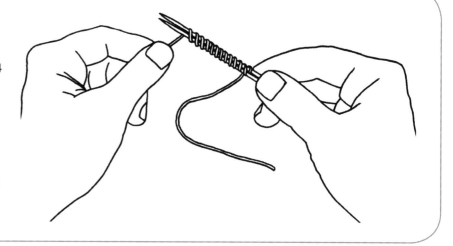

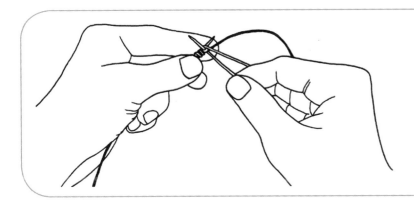

4. Using bottom needle that you pulled through, knit across stitches of top needle.

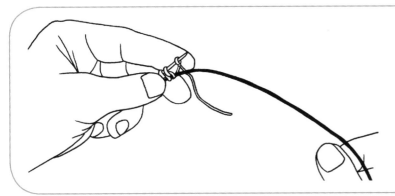

5. Turn the needles 180 degrees so that the top needle with the wraps you just knit across is now on the bottom, pull the cable until the unworked wraps are back on the needle tip. Pull the tip of the bottom needle and slide the stitches onto the cable, drop the slip knot off the end of the top needle and undo it.

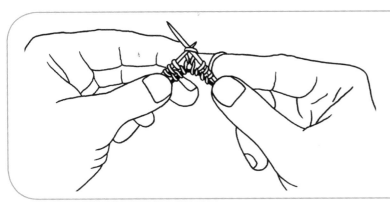

6. Use the bottom needle to knit across the unworked wraps on the top needle, pulling the first stitch tightly to avoid gaping.

7. Knit across both needles once more then begin **Rnd 1** of pattern.

LONG-TAIL CAST-ON

1. Make a slip knot with a long tail–use approximately 1in/2.5cm of yarn per cast on stitch needed. Hold needle with your right hand and with yarn hanging down part the two pieces with your index finger and thumb so that the ball end of the yarn is around your index finger and the long tail is around your left thumb.

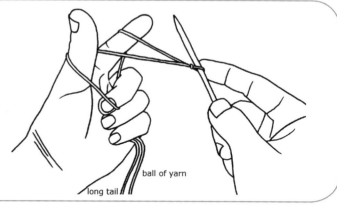

ball of yarn

long tail

2. Bring needle down in front of thumb and insert point under the loop that is wrapped around the thumb.

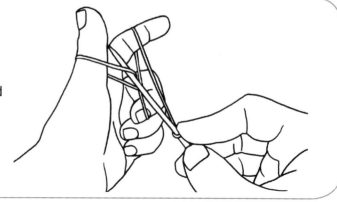

3. Bring the tip of needle over the yarn on the index finger and enter the loop wrapped around that finger from above.

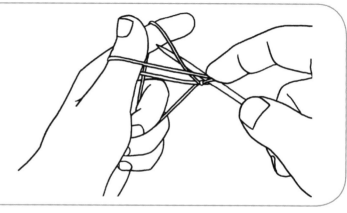

4. Bring the needle back down through the thumb loop. Drop the loop from your thumb to form a new stitch.

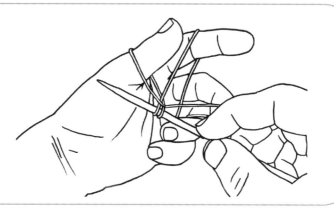

5. Part the yarn with your index finger and thumb again as in step 1; snug the stitch up if it is too loose. Repeat steps 1-5 until the desired number of stitches is reached.

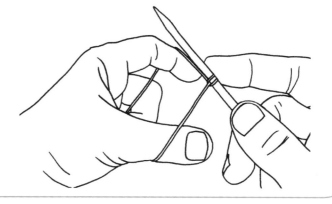

Follow the arrow:

Up the thumb, down the finger, through the middle of the thumb loop, then release the thumb loop.

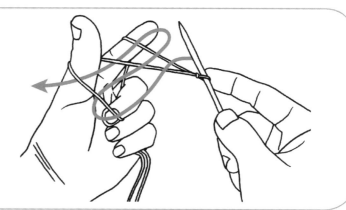

SEWN BIND-OFF

1. Cut a length of yarn 4 times the width of the knitted edge to be bound off, thread the end through a yarn needle.

2. Slip the yarn needle through the first two stitches as if to purl without dropping the stitches from the needle.

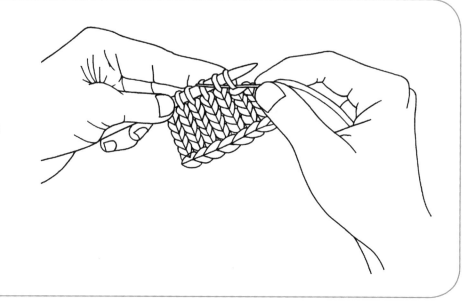

3. Slip the needle back into the first stitch as if to knit, then slip this stitch off the needle.

4. Repeat steps 2 and 3 until all of the stitches have been bound off.

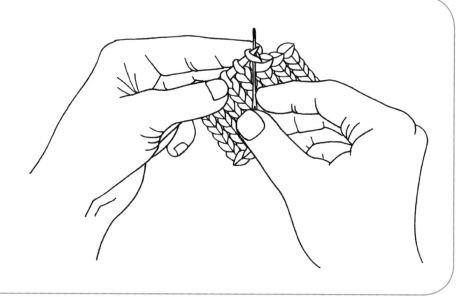

CONTRIBUTORS

styling Shannon Cook & Jane Richmond
photographer Nicholas Kupiak
model Rylee Werbiski
technical editor Kate Atherley
editor Austen Gilliland

THANK-YOUS

We would like to thank the following people for their support in the making of this book:

Kate Atherley, for her wonderful tech editing skills and patience.

Nicholas Kupiak, for his magical photos.

Our testers extraordinare! So many of you put your heart and soul into making our patterns as good as they can be and we couldn't have done it without your endless enthusiasm and support.

Austen Gilliland for being our fabulous eyes behind the scenes and to Barbara Hartmann for her invaluable proof-reading.

Our stunningly gorgeous model Rylee Werbiski. Your natural beauty is so inspiring and you were such a trooper throughout this whole process.

Our knitter friends, for their support, love, laughter and endless friendship.

JANE

To my brother Nicholas for agreeing to yet another year of maddening deadlines and constant pestering about filler shots! This book would be nothing without your involvement and I feel privileged to take this journey with you.

To my friends and family for their constant love and support during these long projects and for putting up with my mini meltdowns, plan canceling, and call screening during the weeks approaching our publishing deadline.

To all of the wonderful knitters who encourage and support me and my work, you are the fuel that keeps me creating and I am so grateful to be part of such a warm and supportive community.

And, last but not least, to Shannon for never letting me walk this road alone. You have been an unconditional friend, a bulletproof business partner, and a beam of light helping me find the road back to myself on my own JOURNEY. Luvs ya!

SHANNON

To my best friend, husband and never-ending supporter, Jeremy. I love you. Thank you for putting up with me and my dreams this past year. You mean the world to me.

To my two little girls–thank you so much for making me smile everyday and for your patience for all those times Mommy couldn't play because she was working.

To my biggest cheerleaders and the best parents–my mom and dad. You listen to me chat for hours and hours about this stuff and I love that I can do it and you always listen. Without you guys my patterns would have copious spelling and grammatical errors.

To my Mom, Nana and Omi–thank you from the bottom of my heart for teaching me the love of handmade.

To my awesome readers and online friends–I adore you all. You have supported me and cheered me on through life's ups and downs and throughout this whole process of making my dreams come true. I truly appreciate each and every one of you for reading, making alongside me, inspiring me and always being there.

And to Jane, my amazingly talented and gorgeous partner in crime, I adore you beyond words. Thank you for everything you have taught me and for the gift of your friendship. There is nobody else that I would rather spend the "witching hours" with.

DIRECTORY

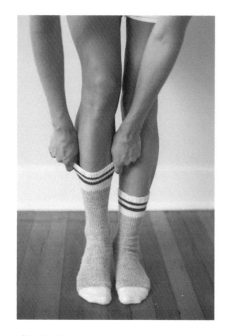

CLIMB
page 80

ONWARD
page 82

SPATE
page 86

SWIFT
page 88

ANTRORSE
page 90

INLAND
page 100

JANE RICHMOND

Jane Richmond lives and works from her home on Vancouver Island. She has been self-publishing her designs since 2008, and most recently has been published in *Cascadia: Knits from the West Coast* (Cooperative Press, 2013).

Known for her classic aesthetic and clearly written patterns, Jane delivers designs that are fun to knit and easy to wear.

WEB || www.janerichmond.com
EMAIL || janerichmonddesigns@gmail.com

SHANNON COOK

Shannon Cook is a blogger, knitting and sewing pattern designer, wife, and mom to two daughters. She is happily living a handmade life near the ocean on Vancouver Island.

Shannon designs patterns for the modern knitter. With their engaging textures, vibrant colours and striking lines, her fun, dynamic garments and accessories are destined to become wardrobe staples.

WEB || www.veryshannon.com
EMAIL || askveryshannon@gmail.com

"Life is a journey, not a destination."

~ Ralph Waldo Emerson

CPSIA information can be obtained
at www.ICGtesting.com
Printed in the USA
LVIW02n1158021213
363154LV00010B/21

* 9 7 8 0 9 9 1 7 2 8 9 1 6 *